Jack's Book of Blessings

Jack's Book of Blessings

Celtic Poems by a Scottie Dog

Beth A. Richardson with Jack the Scottie

To all the dogs
who went before:
Tigger, Spec,
and, especially, Jack.

PREFACE

We had all kinds of plans for this section of the book. I had told Jack that he could write it and he was doing research on other dogs who had written books, but then someone called out, "Squirrell," and he was out the back door again. So it turned out that I chose for myself the honor of writing the preface.

The "Bless to me" form of these poems is of Celtic origin. We find in the oral tradition of the Scottish highlands blessings for every sort of tool and task: from kindling the fire in the morning to smooring the hearth at night. From the birth of a child to the death of an old one. This form—"bless to me"—brings us into the present moment, which is the place our pets live all the time. So Jack's blessings lead us through his day of enjoying each moment: the walk, the leash, the treats, the dog park (and even the not-so-enjoyable bath).

We lost Jack a short time ago to cancer. He was here one day, and then he was just gone. Since then, I've had the most lovely, sad, sweet visits with friends of Jack's who love their canines, felines, and even other species. What is this startling habit we have of throwing ourselves into a love for friends who are bound to leave us way too early? Friends we are never ready to lose. What is this pure, uncomplicated love for beloveds who, we know, will break our hearts. And then, what do we do? We turn right back around and fall helplessly in love again.

This book is for all of us who love, who grieve, and then chose to love again.

Blessings,
Beth A. Richardson
March 3, 2019

BROKEN WIDE OPEN

As soon as we laid eyes on you
Our hearts rushed in, unprotected,
Held captive by you
With your bright, smiling eyes.

Even with your hair grown long
Like a Highland cow
Those brown, trusting eyes,
"They're under there somewhere,"
Reflected love.
Unconditional love,

We fed you, watched you grow,
Cheered your every milestone,
Forgave your every transgression,
(Even that time you unraveled
The Berber carpet in the bedroom.)

We loved you with wild abandon,
Ignoring the certainty
That someday we'd lose you.
And now you have gone.
And our unprotected hearts
Have shattered, quite completely,
Broken wide open by the sudden loss of you.

"Thank you" is all we can say.
Thank you for being our very sweet pup.
Stealer of hearts.
Such a good dog.

Hearts will heal, eventually.
But they will be forever reconfigured
By loving you.

CONTENTS

ACKNOWLEDGMENTS
By Jack the Scottie

(These acknowledgments were written in the enthusiastic voice of Jack, often aided by the influence in spelling, punctuation, and grammar by Arya. Apologies in advance.)

This book could not have been written without Tons of Help. And Thousands of Treats. When Mom said I should Write a Book of Blessings. I just looked at her. But then she said, "There will be Lots of Treats" and I became Very Interested.

I would like to express my gratitude to My Mom who took me for all those walks. And My Mom who fed me. And My Mom who lifted me up on the bed at night and put me down on the floor in the morning. I would like to express my gratitude, also, to My Mom for taking me to the Dog Park and for Dropping Food on the Floor while cooking.

I would be Remiss if I did not also Express my Gratitude to All my Canine Friends in the Neighborhood. To Sweetie, Turbo, Zoe, Darla, Jordan, and Mocha. And, especially Girlfriend (of blessed memory). To my Dog Park friends, Doc and Howard. My People Friends: Deen, John, Sue, Dean, and, especially, Joe, and Peggy (Who have Treats for Me whenever they are home). I would like to thank Sandy, Spec's Mom, who gave me Haircuts and let me run in her Yard and Bark at the Dogs Next Door. I would also like to express my Gratitude to My Friend, Tracy, the founder and proprietor of Camp Tracy and Said, my longest canine friend (besides Spec, of blessed memory). (I can never repay Tracy for all the fun. And Treats.)

To Graford and Fiona Earle, Madison and Jackson Conley Cottingham, Roxie and Bella McKeever-Burgett, Dallas Sears, and Madison Williams-Martin: my dog friends who chewed on the manuscript and offered reviews. And Grayson and Pepper Allen who offered endorsements Even Though They Are Cats!!

This book would Not have been Possible without the Support and Encouragement of my Friends around the World (including Six Cats in Oregon and Auntie Deborah!!!). You have read my Blog Posts, supported me in my Campaign for President of the Back Yard, taken the Flat Jack version of me on Vacation with you All Over the World. You have supported me through My Trials and Cheered my Victories. Most of All, You Have Sent Me Love. And for That, I am Grateful.

P.S. (From Beth) Gratitude for the editing gifts of Roberta Croteau and Lynn Gilliam, the introduction by Roberta Bondi, and the artistic support of the creative folks at Art & Soul, Nashville.

INTRODUCTION
By Roberta Bondi

When Beth asked Curly, my white-haired Bichon Frisée, and me to write a short introduction to Jack's book of blessings, I was excited. I had read his blessings and I loved them. They are such great prayers, which the world always needs, especially in these hard times, but they were also written by a dog. Everybody knows that dogs are especially good at blessing others as well as asking others to bless them. Jack, of course, was always particularly articulate in his own canine way, and as a true lover of God, others, and the everyday world he lived in, he was perfectly suited to write this book.

I knew from the start, however, that there would be problems as I worked with Curly. There were two issues, one of them mechanical. First, Curly has a very hard time with the computer. He doesn't have opposable thumbs and his toes are close together, so he really has trouble typing. On top of this, Curly is a stubborn dog who always wants to do everything "his own self." He could dictate to me, however, and this is how we solved this one.

But there was a far more serious problem arising out of his very nature as a dog. Why would any dog have to ask God to bless anything to him when everybody knows God already blesses dogs—from the many times they wake up during the day till long after they go to sleep at night. Dogs breathe God in with every breath and they never breathe God out at all. Who would believe Jack could have written the book in the first place?

Now, Curly thinks he know everything and he isn't very open minded when it comes to human beings, so it was hardly surprising that I couldn't see how we would be able to overcome this problem. Finally, though, I hit on an idea. I told him I was sure Jack had written his book for us ignorant humans who really needed it. Fortunately, this worked, though I had to promise him all the run-on sentences he wanted, since he loves to run.

Here is Curly's contribution: "This is a good book and everybody should read it unless they are dogs who already know it all and they can't read very well after all and they can always find comic books to peruse— that is a good word, isn't it? The end."

So, here it is. Jack's book in all its splendor. A book of blessings by the great literary master and spiritual teacher, Jack "the Scottie" Richardson.

WALK

Bless to me this walk
That I take
To the park twice a day.

Bless to me the morning,
The smells of last night
And of the new day.

Bless to me each house we pass
And the people who come and go.

Bless to me the street sign
And the fire hydrant,
Multitudes of smells,
Sources of news.

Bless to me all the dogs.
The bunnies, the squirrels,
And especially the cats
Who watch me, but don't let me sniff.

Bless to me the evening,
The mysteries of the creeping shadows
And creatures of the night.

Bless to me our coming home,
The unleashing, the shaking off,
The tasty treat.

Bless to me this walk.

BOWL

Bless to me this bowl
Where my breakfast and supper
Appear each day.

Bless to me
The bowl's coolness against my tongue.
I lick it out several times through the day,
Making sure there's nothing left in it to eat.

Bless to me its shiny emptiness
That mirrors the emptiness of my tummy.

Bless to me my longing looks
At the bowl.
At my mom.
At the bowl.
At my mom.

Come quickly, breakfast.
Come quickly, supper.
Come quickly, food, to my bowl.

Bless to me this bowl.

TREATS

Bless to me the treats,
The tasty morsels
Just for me.

Bless to me the treats.
The kind I get when I "Sit."
The kind I get when I "Stay."
The kind I get when it falls on the floor.

Bless to me the treats,
Savory or sweet,
Soft or chewy,
Every kind of treat, a delight to ingest.

Bless to me the word *Treat*.
When I hear it,
My mouth begins to water.

Bless to me the treats.

SQUIRREL

Bless to me this squirrel
From whom I guard
My family's yard.

Bless to me
Its little nose and curly tail,
Its feet that cling
To bird feeders and branches.

Bless to me
Its taunting grin
As it munches
On seeds outside my door.

Bless to me
Its courage to fly through the air
When I race out the door.

And bless to me
Its courage to return
After I have scared it away.

Bless to me this squirrel.

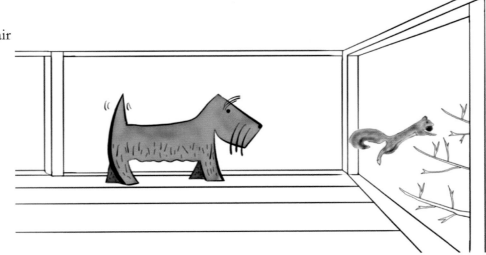

KITCHEN FLOOR

Bless to me this kitchen floor,
The place where I am fed.

Bless to me its soothing flatness
Which welcomes me
To a peaceful nap.

Bless to me this runway to the backyard,
On it I sit or lie or stalk
The squirrels that haunt the porch.

Bless to me this space
Of abundant sustenance,
Mealtime, treats, or family meals,
I watch the floor
For food to appear.
(It always does ... eventually.)

Bless to me this kitchen floor,
The cooks, the food, the family.

Bless to me this kitchen floor.

NAP

Bless to me this morning nap.
After breakfast, walk, and romp.
People all gone,
Time to rest.

Bless to me this afternoon nap.
Spread out on my tummy.
Turned over on my back.
Curled up in my bed.
Quiet interlude.

Bless to me this evening nap.
After dinner, walk, and romp.
People busy, getting sleepy.
Time for bed.

Bless to me this nap.

SQUEAKY TOY

Bless to me this squeaky toy,
Its softness, its funny noises.
When I chew on it, I feel happy.

Bless to me this squeaky toy,
This thing that stays on the floor.
Or in the toy basket.
Or in my bed.
Or tucked under the sofa.
Or wherever I last hid it.

Bless to me this squeaky toy,
That reminds me of something familiar
I can't quite name,
Can't quite remember.
When I chew on it, I feel fierce.

Bless to me this squeaky toy,
New or old,
Torn or whole,
Friend and playmate,
Just for me.

Bless to me this squeaky toy.

LEASH

Bless to me this leash,
This beautiful tether I wear
When I go out with my person.

Bless to me its jingly sound
That I hear from the other room
Letting me know my person is ready
For me to take her somewhere.

Bless to me the excited anticipation
Of walks down the street,
Of trips in the car,
Of visits to the park.

Bless to me each time
We don't end up at The Vet.

Bless to me this leash,
This beautiful tether I wear
When I go out with my person.

Bless to me this leash.

DOG PARK

Bless to me this dog park,
The land where I run free.

Bless to me the car ride,
The race to the gate,
The long, long, long seconds of waiting
For my leash to be removed.

Bless to me the wide-open, spaces.
Each rock and tree,
Each sight and smell and sound
Of people and dogs,
Of dogs and people.

Bless to me the running, the barking.
The chasing and being chased,
The sniffing and being sniffed.

Bless to me each dog I meet
And their person, too.

Bless to me this dog park.

CHAIR (AT THE VET'S)

Bless to me this chair
This strong and safe chair
Under which I hide
At the doctor's office.

Bless to me this chair
And its durable seat
That shelters me from the
Giant vet tech who threatens
To pick me up
And put me on the table.

Bless to me this chair
In its little corner.

And bless to me the treats
I know are in the cabinet.
Come quickly, treats.
Come quickly, come now.

Bless to me this chair.

KITTEN

Bless to me this kitten
Who lives on the other side of the door
At Tracy's house.

Bless to me her smell, her sounds,
Her little paws that torment me.

Bless to me this feline,
So exotic, so elusive,
So familiar, and yet so strange to me.

Bless to me this kitten
Whose paws I touch,
Whose purrs I study.

Bless to me this kitten,
Who lives on the other side of the door
At Tracy's house.

Bless to me this kitten.

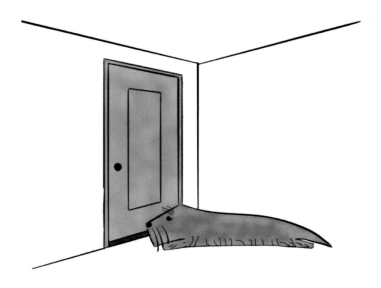

LAP

Bless to me this lap
Upon which I cuddle
In the easy chair.

Bless to me its warmth and comfort,
The soft and gentle pat-pats
As we sit in silence.

Bless to me the hands that pick me up
And place me on the lap,
Even when I pretend I'd rather not.

Bless to me the respite
From the hazards of the floor,
The barking, nipping, and aggravation of my sister.

Bless to me this lap
And the one who invites me here.

Bless to me this lap.

WINDOW SEAT

Bless to me this window seat
With a view of the driveway, the yard,
And the whole neighborhood.

Bless to me the things I see.
Neighbor dogs running across my yard.
Cats sneaking through the bushes.
Children walking to the park.

Bless to me the things I hear.
Dogs barking, birds singing,
People making people noises.

Bless to me the soft pillows upon the bench,
The window sill where I rest my head,
The sounds and smells that come to me
Even when I doze for a while.

Bless to me this window seat
From which I keep an eye on my domain.

Bless to me this window seat.

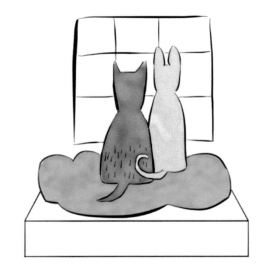

BATH

Bless to me this bath.
I hate it, and yet
When I'm clean I feel so good.

Bless to me the warmth of the water,
The gentle words and hands
Of the one who keeps me in the tub.

Bless to me the spray
That gets the soap out of my beard.

Bless to me the towels
That let me know the bath is over,
The tender way Mom dries my feet.

Bless to me the open door,
My refreshing, boisterous run
Through the house,
Celebrating the end of the bath,
Reveling in my wet cleanness.

Bless to me this bath.

ARYA (MY SISTER)

Bless to me my Arya
Who came to me
As a lost and homeless puppy.

Bless to me her perky ears,
Her curvy tail,
Her long, tall legs.

Bless to me her puppy-ness
That entertains me
When I have nothing to do.

Bless to me her bossiness
When she tries to herd me
Down the street or across the room.

Bless to me my Arya,
Who is no longer a puppy,
But still, my very own dog.

Bless to me my Arya.

BED

Bless to me this bed,
The people's bed upon which I sleep
When I'm not too dirty or wet.

Bless to me this quiet time,
This safety, this luxury,
The warmth of my pack,
Settled in for the night.

Bless to me the lifting up at night
And the setting down in the morning.

Bless to me the blankets
And pillows
Upon which I curl.

Bless to me the warmth
Of feet or legs or hip
Against which I nestle.
And the person on top of which I shiver
During thunderstorms.

Bless to me this bed,
This special family time,
These tender hours of love.

Bless to me this bed.

ABOUT THE AUTHORS

Beth A. Richardson, is a writer, photographer, editor, cartoonist, and lover of dogs. She is the author of a companion book to *Jack's Book of Blessings* called *Christ Beside Me, Christ Within Me: Celtic Blessings* published by The Upper Room, Nashville, TN.

Jack, a Scottish Terrier, was born in Indiana and lived with Beth and her family in Nashville, Tennessee. Jack the Scottie was a "real dog," despite the cartoons included herein. (Cartoon Jack was much more cooperative than "real Jack.") Jack passed away suddenly in October of 2018. He lives on in the hearts of many.

You'll find stories, poems, and reflections inspired by their life together on the blogs, jackthescottie.com and betharichardson.com. Jack the Scottie greeting cards are available from Redbubble.com.

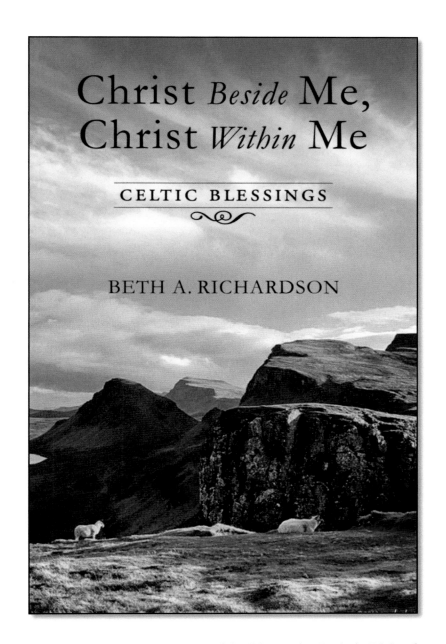

Christ Beside Me, Christ Within Me: Celtic Blessings by Beth A. Richardson

PRAISE FROM CATS AND DOGS

At last! A book that goes beyond affirming we non-humans bless God, to one that translates those blessings! Jack's Scottish Celtic heritage proves ideal for framing this universal expression of praise. As a Norwegian Forest cat, my prayers are more reserved than Jack's, and I certainly do not have his sort of co-dependent relationship with my humans ("Mom," p. 3, really?!). But the nap, the bed, the treats, the lap, these are universal in relationships with domesticated humans, every one of whom should read this book to strengthen their often inconstant faith.
- **Pepper** Allen, Norwegian Forest cat

Jack has penned such lovely blessings for the life of us dogs. We treasure all the things that matter--our families, our food, the smells, the walks. Jack rocks!
- **Graford** and **Fiona** Earle, border collies

Jack's Book of Blessings is the perfect pause from our barking and licking and jumping and growling to remember that this life is a gift, and we are glad to be living it. Do yourself a favor, take a pause from your dog life and enjoy these nuggets of love!
- **Roxy** and **Bella** McKeever-Burgett, dachshunds

"I give it 5 paws." "I give it 5 licks but Mom said no chews."
- **Jackson** and **Madison** Conley Cottingham, maltipoos

Jack's book of blessings receives two paws up.
- **Grayson** (Feline)

I enjoyed sniffing and chewing on this book! My person tried to read it to me but we didn't get very far. Every time I heard the word, treat, I lost focus and couldn't pay attention to anything else. My person tried to keep going but I'm still waiting for my treat. I'm a big guy. I need my treats! Anyway, any book that talks about treats is a good one in my view. Two giant paws up from me! Can I have a treat now?
- **Dallas** Sears

If humans could see the world as Jack saw it, life would probably give them more treats and belly rubs.
- **Madison** Williams-Martin

Made in the USA
Monee, IL
15 October 2020

45066211R10031